EXTREMELY GROSS ANIMALS

Stinky, Slimy and Strange Animal Adaptations

Claire Eamer

Kids Can Press

To all the kids who delight in grossness. (Me, too!) — C.E.

Published in Canada and the U.S. by Kids Can Press Ltd.
25 Dockside Drive, Toronto, ON M5A 0B5

Kids Can Press is a Corus Entertainment Inc. company
www.kidscanpress.com

The artwork in this book was rendered digitally.
The text is set in Officina Sans.

Edited by Stacey Roderick
Designed by Barb Kelly
Photo research by Kathleen Keenan and Olga Kidisevic

Printed and bound in Dongguan, Guangdong, P.R. China,
in 10/2020 by Toppan Leefung

CM 21 0 9 8 7 6 5 4 3 2 1

FSC
www.fsc.org
MIX
Paper from
responsible sources
FSC® C104723

Library and Archives Canada Cataloguing in Publication

Title: Extremely gross animals : stinky, slimy and strange animal adaptations / written by Claire Eamer.
Names: Eamer, Claire, 1947– author.
Description: Includes bibliographical references and index.
Identifiers: Canadiana 20200237179 | ISBN 9781525303371 (hardcover)
Subjects: LCSH: Animals — Adaptation — Juvenile literature.
Classification: LCC QL49 .E36 2021 | DDC j591.4 — dc23

Kids Can Press gratefully acknowledges that the land on which our office is located is the traditional territory of many nations, including the Mississaugas of the Credit, the Anishnabeg, the Chippewa, the Haudenosaunee and the Wendat peoples, and is now home to many diverse First Nations, Inuit and Métis peoples.

We thank the Government of Ontario, through Ontario Creates; the Ontario Arts Council; the Canada Council for the Arts; and the Government of Canada for supporting our publishing activity.

Contents

Welcome to the Wild World of Gross!

Some animals are cute and cuddly, such as puppies and kittens, and others are fierce and majestic, such as lions and polar bears. Some animals are ugly, some are scary and some are dangerous. But the animals in this book? They're just plain gross.

These animals wallow in snot or cover themselves with vomit. They spit and fart and spew. They gobble up poop or feed it to their babies. They turn other animals into zombie slaves. Some even abandon pieces of their own bodies to escape predators. Blech!

In this book, we look at the grossest of the gross — animals that can disgust even the most loyal animal lover. And we'll see how those habits, as revolting as they might seem, are actually amazing survival skills. In fact, in nature, it's often **survival of the grossest!**

Gross or Not-So-Gross?

An animal that eats poop — known as feces in more polite company — doesn't consider it icky or disgusting. Nor does an animal that willingly covers itself in snot. So why are we humans grossed out by it?

In part, it's because we're taught to be. From the time we're babies, we're told that some things are gross and disgusting. And it's a good lesson to learn since babies put everything they can reach into their mouths, including things that can make them sick.

But our sense of what is gross isn't entirely learned. For example, to us humans, poop and vomit smell awful. So do moldy fruit and rotting meat. The smell of these things can make us feel queasy or dizzy — which are physical responses — so we avoid them. And avoiding them is generally a good idea since all those things can make us sick. In fact, this useful sense of disgust might well have developed over millions of years of evolution because it helped keep humans alive.

But what disgusts us doesn't necessarily disgust the animals in this book. Many of these animals actually *survive* on revolting substances and *thrive* on gross habits. Once you take a closer look, what's revolting and gross is often pretty fascinating. You might even find the disgusting creatures in this book a bit less revolting once you get to know them.

So, hold your nose and dive right in!

One Person's ICK
Is Another Person's Treasure

Not everyone agrees on what's icky. In fact, what grosses you out can depend on what you are used to. For example, how do you feel about eating insects? At least a quarter of the people in the world happily chow down on bugs. In Thailand, you can buy spiced, roasted grasshoppers at street food stalls. For many Indigenous Australians, witchetty grubs — basically caterpillars — picked fresh off the bush are a treat. And in North America, cricket protein powder is sold in grocery stores.

Yuck!

The Scoop on Poop

Poop — also known as feces, dung, scat, droppings and, of course, poo — contains stuff a body needs to get rid of, from dead blood cells and digestive microbes to food that wasn't absorbed by the digestive system. Imagine how much poop all the creatures on this planet produce every day! We should be buried in the stuff, but we aren't — thanks, in large part, to dung beetles.

Dung Like Dinner

Worldwide, there are somewhere between 9000 and 10 000 species of dung beetles. For these beetles, poop is everything. They feast on it, they nest in it, and they lay their eggs and tend their young in it.

Dung beetles' sensitive antennae pick up the scent of fresh dung and guide them to the source. What they do then depends on which kind of dung beetle they are: roller, tunneler or dweller.

The **roller** beetles are among the strongest animals in the world relative to their size. A male or female (depending on the species) molds fresh dung into a ball that can weigh 50 times more than the beetle itself. After rolling the ball a short distance away from the dung pile, the beetle sends out pheromones — chemical messages — to attract a mate. Together, the two beetles roll the dung ball farther away and dig an underground nest. They put the dung ball in the nest, the female lays an egg inside the ball, and they cover the whole thing up. When the larva hatches from the egg, it begins to eat its way through the dung ball. By the time it has finished its food supply, it's a full-grown adult beetle.

Tunnelers take a different approach. They set up camp either under or at the edge of a dung pile and tunnel into the earth beneath it. They lay their eggs in the tunnels along with stashes of dung, so when the larvae hatch, dinner is already on the table.

The last group of dung beetles, the **dwellers**, are much more casual. Some species arrive at a pile of fresh dung, take a sip or two of the dung fluid, drop off a few eggs and leave. Others will burrow into the dung to lay their eggs.

But whether it's carried away and buried by rollers, buried by tunnelers or eaten on the spot by dwellers, by the time dung beetles are done with a poo pile, most of it will be gone.

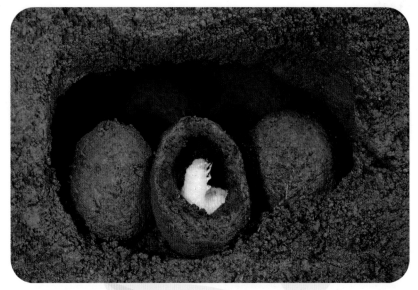

Dung beetle larva inside its dung ball home

Dung-licious!

Eating poop is a common practice in the animal world, and with good reason. Even though it has already passed through one digestive system, dung is still full of nutrients. Most plant-eating animals get only 10 to 30 percent of the nutrients out of their food before pooping out what's left. Plenty of animals — not just dung beetles — are willing to make sure those leftovers don't go to waste.

Scat Tricks

Insects are the most common fans of poop, but they're not the only ones. And while most animals come for the buffet, a few have other uses for the stuff.

Feasting on Seconds

The insect-eating grotto salamander (*Eurycea spelaea*) spends its whole life in caves in the Ozark Mountains of the southeastern United States. But not many insects venture into the caves, unless they are swept in with surface water. Fortunately, something else lives in the caves: gray bats.

After nights out bug hunting, the bats spend their days resting. And pooping. Bats don't keep food in their bodies for long because it makes them heavy for flying, so their poop is full of half-digested bits of insects — a banquet for hungry grotto salamanders.

Mmm, bat poop!

Baby Food

Baby elephants eat elephant dung. Why? Because their mothers feed it to them. It's not as gross as it sounds, though. For one thing, an elephant's digestive system isn't very efficient, so elephant poop is full of seeds, nuts and half-digested grass and leaves. More importantly, the dung of an adult elephant contains gut microbes — tiny organisms that help elephants digest plants — which the baby will need once it's no longer living only on its mother's milk. Elephants aren't the only animals to feed their babies poop. So do rabbits, pandas and koalas, among others.

Poop Imposter

Australian bird-dropping spiders (*Celaenia excavata*) don't so much as use poop as pretend to be poop. They are quite large for spiders, plenty big enough to make a good meal for a bird or wasp. Fortunately, the spiders hunt at night, when birds and wasps aren't out. And during the day, they settle on a leaf or branch with their legs tucked under their bodies. Their black, gray and white markings and lumpy shape make them look like a pile of unappetizing bird droppings rather than a fat, tasty spider.

Mucus Madness

Hagfish mouth

If you've ever had a really bad cold (and who hasn't?), you probably felt as if you were drowning in snot. But that's nothing compared to a hagfish. The hagfish is a mucus *machine*!

Snot Pretty

The hagfish is just as unlovely as its name. It's a pinkish, eel-like animal with no jaw, no working eyes and a couple of tongues. A hagfish eats marine worms and dead things from the seabed — often burrowing right into the corpses to get to the really good stuff. And as if that's not enough to put you off, the hagfish, when threatened, produces slime. Lots of slime.

The clear, gooey stuff pours off their bodies by the bucketful in less than a second. So gross but so effective! Any fish that hopes to make a meal of a hagfish will find its mouth and gills instantly clogged with slime. Hagfish slime has even driven sharks away.

This amount of slime could smother the slime machine itself, except that hagfish have come up with a solution. The hagfish makes a loop with its body, squeezes its head through the loop and runs the resulting knot down the length of its body to scrape off the slime.

While hagfish slime might sound disgusting, it's actually amazing. It contains two main things: thread-like protein fibers (which are wound up like balls of yarn within a cell) and mucus. When the hagfish feels threatened (and, apparently, almost anything feels threatening to a hagfish), its slime glands

Hagfish slime

push out the balls of fiber and the mucus. The cell walls around the protein fibers dissolve as soon as they hit the seawater. The protein fibers unwind, tangling around each other and trapping water and mucus in an explosion of slime. And all this happens in just a fraction of a second.

The fibers are stronger than nylon but so thin that it would take up to 20 of them to equal the thickness of a silkworm thread. Some scientists are studying hagfish slime as a natural replacement for petroleum-based fibers to make superlight, superstrong fabrics. Hagfish-slime shirt, anyone?

What Is Mucus?

Mucus is a mixture of gooey fluid, protein strands that make the gooey stuff stick together even better and an assortment of cells caught up in the guck. Humans produce up to a liter and a half (a little less than half a gallon) of mucus a day. Some of it covers and protects sensitive tissue, such as the lining of our noses, while the rest trickles down our throats to protect lung surfaces and the tissues of the digestive tract. We need *some* mucus to stay healthy — but thankfully not as much as a hagfish produces.

Snotty and Snottier

So, human snot and hagfish slime are useful, as well as disgusting. Some other ways animals use mucus are also useful but not *quite* so gross. Then again, it *is* still snot.

Sleeping Beauty

A parrotfish lives a pleasant life. It spends its days scraping food — algae and tiny animals — off the coral reefs of the world's warm oceans. At night, the parrotfish stays safe and cozy, completely enclosed in a special kind of sleeping bag made of mucus, spewed fresh each night from glands near its gills. Why? It's hard to get a straight answer from a fish, but one theory is that the mucus keeps out tiny blood-sucking parasites that attack reef fish at night. It might also warn the parrotfish that a predator is close when it bumps into the slime. Or it's possible that the mucus makes it hard for predators to smell the parrotfish.

Undercover Fish

Almost everyone has seen a picture of a clownfish, the little orange fish with white and black stripes that hangs out among the poisonous tentacles of a sea anemone. Yet the anemone doesn't sting the clownfish, and the clownfish will even defend the anemone against other fish. One theory about how this puzzling relationship works is that it depends on the layer of mucus that coats the clownfish. The mucus might act as an armor that blocks the anemone's stingers. Or it might work like a disguise so the anemone doesn't recognize the fish as either food or an enemy.

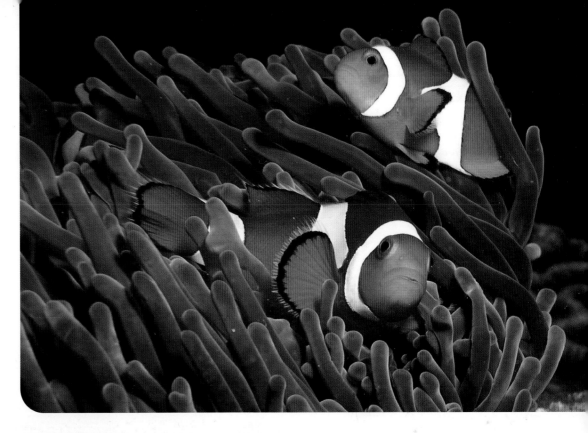

Violet sea snail

Mucus raft

Snot Sailor

The violet sea snail (*Janthina janthina*), also called the purple bubble raft snail, floats around the ocean by hanging upside down from a raft it creates out of bubbles of mucus. If it ever let go, the sea snail would sink and drown, but fortunately, its single foot is stuck firmly to its bubble raft. The violet sea snail's life is spent drifting wherever the wind and currents take it and eating surface-dwelling jellyfish. The female snail gives birth in the open ocean to tiny, perfect replicas of itself: little violet sea snails that can build their own small mucus-bubble rafts right away and set off to drift the seas.

Spit It Out!

Spitting in public is rude and disgusting and unsanitary, right? After all, no one wants to step in someone else's gob of saliva. But some animals have turned spitting into a lethal weapon. Consider, for example, the velvet worm.

Spitting Glue

Gram for gram, velvet worms might be the world's champion spitters. Most velvet worms are about the size of the average earthworm, but they can spit a distance of up to six times their body length. And not only that — instead of saliva, the velvet worm spits glue.

Despite their name, velvet worms aren't actually worms. With anywhere from 13 to 43 pairs of stumpy legs, they look a bit like caterpillars but are actually a small, distinct group of animals that live in the leaf litter and rotting wood of warm, damp forests. Tiny projections called papillae cover their skin and give it a look like velvet. They also have two large papillae, one on each side of the mouth.

At night, velvet worms come out of their hiding places and plod through the undergrowth, searching for insects and other small creatures to eat. They're slow and can barely see, but their skin and antennae are

A magnified look at the papillae on a velvet worm's skin

extremely sensitive. When a velvet worm senses movement, it rears up and spits a glue-like substance out of the two large papillae near its mouth.

The stream of glue comes out fast, making both papillae wave around like uncontrolled fire hoses. This spreads the stuff widely in the direction of the prey, so the velvet worm doesn't need to aim too carefully. The glue starts drying midair and forms sticky strands that tangle around the prey and then trap it as the glue hardens. At its leisure, the velvet worm bites the trapped animal and injects digestive saliva that softens the prey's tissue. Once the internal tissues are pretty much liquid, the velvet worm sucks them out. Velvet worms often top their meals off by eating the glue, which is full of the proteins needed to make more glue.

Velvet worms have been around since long before dinosaurs roamed Earth, so clearly their glue spitting works. Even if it isn't very polite.

A velvet worm mid-spit

Physics and the Velvet Worm

Some Chilean physicists were interested in how fluids behave — and since velvet worm glue starts out as a fluid, they recorded videos of velvet worms spraying. Because the spray takes no more than a fraction of a second, they slowed the video down to see exactly how the papillae work. The force of the fluid being pushed through them causes the papillae to wave back and forth, spraying out streams of tiny glue droplets. Inspired, the scientists are now developing hoses as small as the velvet worm's papillae to make their own tiny droplets for use in nanotechnology, the branch of engineering that deals with things as small as an atom or a molecule.

More Spitters

No other animal has air-hardening spit, but there are plenty of other spitters in the animal world. And sometimes the spittiest-looking spit isn't spit at all.

Water Pistol Sniper

The archerfish spits water with pinpoint accuracy. Archerfish live in the warm waters of southern Asia and northern Australia. There, they lurk near overhanging branches or reeds, waiting for insects to wander into view. When one does, the archerfish aims its pointy snout and unleashes a shot worthy of a sniper. The stream of water shoots up to 2 meters (6.5 feet) with enough force to knock a stunned insect into the water. Sounds simple? Not really. The archerfish has to take physics into account: light bends when it moves between air and water, so the target isn't exactly where the eye says it is, and gravity pulls the water jet down slightly. Yet these fish can hit their prey in about a tenth of the time it takes you to blink your eye! And to top it off, by the time the bug hits the water, the archerfish is already there, waiting for it.

Chemical Warfare

Musk mare is another name for the northern two-striped walking stick, an insect from the southern United States that looks a bit like an arrangement of twigs. When it feels threatened, the musk mare spits a nasty fluid from glands just behind its head, aiming for the eyes of its enemy. The spray can travel at least the length of your arm and causes severe pain. Even if it misses the eyes, being hit anywhere with musk mare spray could make anyone lose interest in bugs. One unlucky bug enthusiast said it was like being zapped with pepper spray.

Bubble Bath

Have you ever come across what looks like a great glob of white foamy spit stuck on a plant or clump of grass? Maybe you thought, "Ugh! Gross!" Well, it's maybe not quite as gross as you thought. Those clumps of foam are made by the nymphs (or juveniles) of spittlebugs, insects that eat the sap and juices of plants. The nymphs are easy prey for birds and other insects, so they hide in bubble shelters. To make the bubbles, they pee out semi-digested plant sap and mix it with mucus made by glands in their abdomens. Then they pump air into the mixture through a canal in their abdomens, creating a mound of foamy bubbles that *looks* like a gob of spit ... but isn't.

Gas Attack

We humans can make some pretty bad smells. Garlic breath, for example. Or gym-sock reek. And nothing can beat a really good fart for clearing the room. But when it comes to gas attacks, we're amateurs compared to the champion of stink warfare — the bombardier beetle.

Chemical Factory

The bombardier beetle can be found on every continent except Antarctica. Bombardier beetles have almost no predators, and with good reason — they look inoffensive enough, but they're actually walking chemical bomb factories.

Most species have orange or brown bodies and limbs, with dark green or brown wing covers. They amble through the undergrowth, looking for smaller insects to eat. They don't look dangerous, but when a bombardier beetle feels threatened, it can unleash a gas attack that would drive a skunk away and even kill smaller enemies.

The bombardier beetle's abdomen contains two glands. One gland holds two chemicals that are kept separated. The other holds a catalyst, a substance that sets off chemical reactions. When the beetle is threatened, both glands empty into a single chamber, which triggers a superfast chemical reaction — basically an explosion.

This explosion in the beetle's abdomen creates a nasty, stinky substance called benzoquinone, as well as water that's been heated to boiling point by the chemical reaction. The pressure of the expanding liquid and steam forces out a fine, scalding-hot and absolutely foul-smelling spray through a flexible nozzle in the beetle's butt. The beetle can aim the spray pretty well anywhere, even forward over its own head. Some kinds of bombardier beetles can blast 20 rounds of spray before running out of ammo.

Imagine you're a shrew thinking about a bombardier beetle dinner. Have you lost your appetite yet?

Toad You Not to Eat That!

Most animals leave bombardier beetles alone, but apparently, some toads can't resist them. Japanese researchers captured toads and bombardier beetles to see what would happen when they met. The toads happily gulped the beetles down so quickly that the beetles had no time to react. But that wasn't the end of the encounter. The beetles set off their chemical bombs inside the toads' stomachs. The scientists could even hear the explosions! Not every toad upchucked as a result — some appear to like their food extra-spicy — but plenty of them did. Amazingly, the vomited-up beetles walked away, apparently unharmed.

Hold Your Nose!

There are plenty of animals that make or use bad smells as a survival trick. Most don't create actual explosions like the bombardier beetle, but their stink attacks are still effective — and gross.

Stand Back!

Fulmars are large seabirds that nest on cliffs high above northern oceans. When nesting, their main defense against predators — mostly other birds and humans — is to projectile-vomit a truly awful-smelling oil. Fulmar chicks are born with the ability to vomit the nasty stuff and will even spew it at their own parents until they learn to recognize them as the birds that bring them food. Besides smelling terrible, the oil sticks to the feathers of attacking birds, making it difficult to fly. Some even drown in the sea below if they can't clean enough oil off their feathers to float.

Rolling Out the "Unwelcome" Mat

The rainbow pitta is a small bird native to Australia's tropical forests. It has beautiful, brightly colored feathers — and very smelly ideas about home decorating. After building its dome-shaped nest, complete with a side entrance hole, the rainbow pitta collects wallaby dung from the surrounding forest. It uses the poop to make a sort of "unwelcome" mat for brown tree snakes, which are very fond of pitta eggs. These snakes hunt by smell, so when one slithers near a dung-adorned nest, all it smells is wallaby poop, not tasty bird egg. And the rainbow pitta's eggs stay safe.

The King of Stink

Say hello to the zorilla (*Ictonyx striatus*) — just keep a safe distance. The zorilla, or striped polecat, lives in Africa's open forests and grasslands. With its long black hair and white patches and stripes, you might think it's an African skunk, especially since zorillas also spray a sticky, foul-smelling liquid out of their anal glands. They sound awfully similar, but recent genetic studies show that the two aren't even distant cousins. Zorillas are actually more closely related to weasels and badgers. And according to disgusted observers, they actually smell worse than skunks. Zorilla spray, which can spread for hundreds of meters or yards, has even driven away lions!

23

Ew... Just Ew!

There's gross — and then there's grosser. In fact, more than a few animals do things that might really make you want to throw up. And speaking of throwing up, let's talk about frogs.

Froggy Feels Sick

Imagine life as an American bullfrog. You're big, you're tough, you're pretty much the boss frog, at least in North America. You lurk among the reeds at the edge of a pond or just below the water's surface and wait for a tasty bug or other small animal to pass by. Then you leap and snap it up with your long, sticky tongue.

Sometimes, though, that long, sticky tongue sucks back something unwelcome or inedible, such as a poisonous insect. That's when the bullfrog pukes its guts out. Literally. Bullfrogs can vomit up their *entire* stomachs.

Blah!

When a frog does this, the stomach doesn't separate from its owner. It stays attached to the frog's innards and hangs out of the frog's mouth, inside out. Most of the contents just fall out, but whatever is left, the frog takes care of. It carefully wipes the stomach off with its right hand, stuffs the whole thing back in its mouth and swallows it back down. The stomach settles into place, somewhat the better for a thorough cleaning.

Why the right hand? Are all bullfrogs right-handed? Frogs' stomachs aren't quite centered in their bodies and dangle out of the right side of the froggy mouth. Frogs have short arms — too short to reach all the way across the mouth — so they have no choice but to use the right hand for stomach-wiping.

Bullfrogs aren't the only frogs that can puke up their stomachs. So can most of a large group called ranid frogs, which live in North America and across the northern parts of Eurasia. Interestingly, the African clawed frog, which belongs to an entirely different group, can also eject its stomach.

Ranid frog

African clawed frog

Swish and Rinse

Animals other than frogs also practice this kind of extreme vomiting. A few kinds of fish — such as rays and sharks — are known to puke up their stomachs. They appear to rinse their stomachs in seawater by shaking them around before swallowing them back down again. It happens very quickly, though. Scientists recorded a reef shark in the Caribbean Sea puking out its stomach and sucking it back in less than half a second.

Reef shark

The ICK Factor

Extreme puking is just one of many unsettling habits found in the animal world. Here are a few more gross-out champions.

Who Needs a Hankie?

Giraffes are champion droolers, with long, drippy tongues — about half a meter (20 inches) long — that are designed to wrap around tree leaves and rip them off branches. Thick, sticky saliva helps the giraffe grip the leaves and also makes them easier to swallow. A bit gross, but not super-gross, right? Well, consider this: a giraffe can wrap that long, flexible tongue around its muzzle and poke it into its own nostrils to clean out its nose. Don't try *that* at home!

SLURP!

Vulture Be Vultching

Just about everything about vultures is gross. They eat rotting flesh. Sometimes they eat so much that they can't even move. They also poop on themselves — although scientists aren't sure why. According to one theory, it's to cool off. Vultures don't have sweat glands, but when the runny waste evaporates, it draws heat away from the birds' legs and feet. According to another theory, the excrement might kill off parasites and diseases picked up while the vultures are walking around on dead things. It's hard to imagine, but vulture poop might be cleaner than the vulture diet.

Poop

SLURP!

The Fly in the Soup

Flies are mostly a nuisance, right? They buzz around the house or your picnic lunch, zipping away just as you're about to swat them. But that's not all. When flies land on your food, they vomit on it! Puked-up digestive juices and saliva help break food down into a soupy substance they can suck through their straw-shaped mouth parts. The problem is that they leave behind some of that fly puke soup for us to share. Flies also eat feces, so they often deposit some bacteria picked up from that as well. So if a fly has landed on your sandwich, you might want to think twice about your next bite.

Didn't Need It Anyway

For humans, throwing away bits of our bodies is generally considered a bad idea, possibly even life-threatening. But for some animals, it's just business as usual. In fact, for the sea cucumber, discarding bits of its body can save its life.

Gutless Wonder

Sea cucumbers spend most of their time creeping slowly along the seabed, looking — as their name suggests — like slightly animated cucumbers. They have a mouth end for sucking up algae, a tube-shaped body for all the usual body functions and a rear end for getting rid of unneeded stuff. Some sea cucumbers have fancy projections and bright colors, but many of them just look like muddy, squashy cucumbers.

However, to fish, octopuses, crabs and plenty of other sea creatures, sea cucumbers look like a delicious lunch.

Unlike its vegetable namesake, though, a sea cucumber can defend itself — and in a thoroughly gross way. When under attack, the animal expels its innards — guts and all. Sea cucumber guts are spewable because its internal organs are attached to the wall of its body in only a few places. When it's time, the attachment points soften and the muscles of the body wall tighten up to turn its innards into ... er ... outards.

Some kinds of sea cucumbers shoot their internal organs out through their mouths, while for others, it's the rear exit. Another type pushes its insides out through a weak spot in the side of its body. However it happens, though, the startled predator is left with a nasty mess that no longer looks quite so delicious. In some cases, it's even poisonous.

While the predator is still getting over the shock, the outside of the sea cucumber creeps away and holes up to recover. Amazingly, the animals can regenerate, or recreate, all their missing organs! Some species need several months to regenerate completely, but others are back to normal in as little as a week.

Chocolate chip sea cucumber foraging at the bottom of the sea

28

How Sea Cucumbers Rebuild Their Innards

Sea cucumbers are wizards at rebuilding themselves. Sometimes, the remaining bits of sea cucumber guts simply grow longer and longer until they reach from mouth to anus again. If there's nothing left of the original guts, other kinds of cells clump together at the wound, change into the right kind of cells and grow into a brand-new working digestive tract.

More Bits and Bodies

Not many animals play as fast and loose with bits of their bodies as the sea cucumber, but quite a few have body parts or substances they seem able to do without. And some take things to the absolute extreme ...

A Tale of a Tail

Most lizards can discard their tails in order to escape predators. Usually, dropped lizard tails continue to wriggle briefly in order to distract the predator, but the chameleon gecko (*Carphodactylus laevis*), which lives in the forests of northeastern Australia, takes things a bit further. Its tail wriggles, flops about and even *squeaks*! What predator could resist that? Meanwhile, the chameleon gecko scoots away to safety and begins growing a new tail.

Squeak!

Squeak!

A Bloody Shot!

Horned lizards look like pudgy miniature dragons, all spikes and claws. They make a tasty, if slightly prickly, mouthful for predators in the deserts where they live. But they have a very special defense. They chase predators away by shooting blood from their eyes. Well, really, it comes from pouches just below their eyes. They usually wait until a predator is about to take a bite, then fill its mouth with foul-tasting blood. The horrible taste lasts for at least 15 minutes, leaving the lizard plenty of time to escape. The loss of blood doesn't seem to affect the horned lizards at all.

The End of the Tale

Some animals give up parts of their bodies to save themselves, but the Malaysian exploding ant (*Colobopsis explodens*) is truly a team player: some of these exploding ants sacrifice their whole bodies for the sake of the colony. When faced with an invader, the ants use their jaws and legs to grab on tight to the predator. Then the ants squeeze their own rear body segments so hard that they explode, spraying the enemy with smelly, sticky yellow goo that's nasty enough to drive it away or even kill it. The exploding ants die, but their colony survives.

Monster Attack

Zombies, vampires, the undead and the half-dead: they're all popular characters in fiction. But in the animal world, they're the real deal. And the master monsters are parasites — animals, such as the horsehair worm, that survive by using other animals' living (or mostly living) bodies.

Dive, Grasshopper, Dive!

Horsehair worms are long, skinny worms that look a lot like the coarse hair of a horse's mane or tail. In fact, when the wriggly worms kept showing up in horse troughs, people thought they were seeing hair that had somehow come to life. But what they were actually seeing is just as strange: these worms are zombie masters.

Adult horsehair worms live and lay their eggs in water. Sometimes a tiny swimming larva that hatches from a worm's eggs is swallowed by a grasshopper, mantis or other suitable insect that has come to drink from the water. The lucky larva has found its new home, but the insect isn't so lucky.

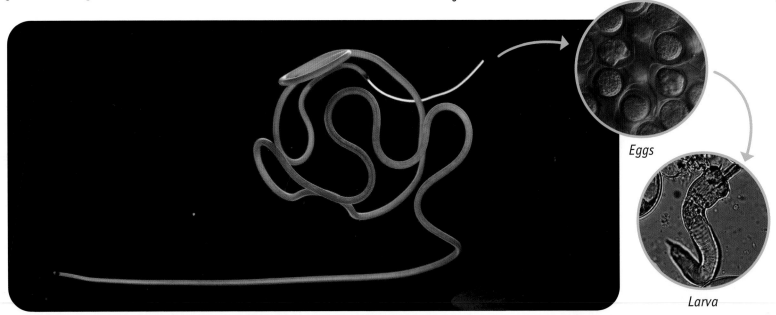

Eggs

Larva

A horsehair worm laying a string of white eggs

The larva breaks through the insect's gut into its body cavity to feed on tissues and blood. Eventually, the larva grows into a long, skinny worm that lives tangled all through the host insect's body. An insect as small as a cricket can be home to a horsehair worm as long as a brand-new pencil. Or longer.

Once the worm is fully grown, though, it needs to return to water. That's when it takes control of its host's mind.

Zombified, the insect searches out water, often jumping in and drowning. This suits the worm just fine as it wriggles out of the insect's body and squirms away in search of a mate to create a new generation of zombie master worms.

This is how horsehair worms seem to appear magically in ponds and troughs — or even in toilets and sinks if the host insects have moved indoors. They have been delivered by zombie express!

A dead mantis with a horsehair worm coiled up inside

Bloodsuckers and Sapsuckers

A parasite is an organism that lives on or in another organism (its host) and gets its food from that organism. Only a few parasites are zombification experts like the horsehair worm. Lice, ticks and fleas are all non-zombifying parasites that live off other animals — including us! There are even plant parasites that live off other plants. Mistletoe — the plant best known as a Christmas decoration — is a parasite that wraps itself around a tree branch and sucks water and nutrients from its host tree.

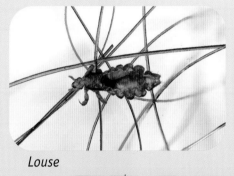

Louse

Tick

Flea

33

Brains and More

Sometimes you don't have to take over the whole creature to get what you want. For most parasites, a little can go a long way.

Say What?

The tongue-eating louse (*Cymothoa exigua*) is more vampire than zombifier. The little crustacean doesn't need its host's brain — just its tongue and a steady supply of blood. A young tongue-eating louse will enter a fish's body through the gills and attach itself to the artery at the base of the fish's tongue. There, it drinks blood from the artery. The fish's tongue withers and dies without its blood supply, but the tongue-eating louse grows to fill the space. It continues living there, feeding on blood as well as loose food particles from the fish's meals. Surprisingly, the fish seems completely unaware that there's an alien in its mouth.

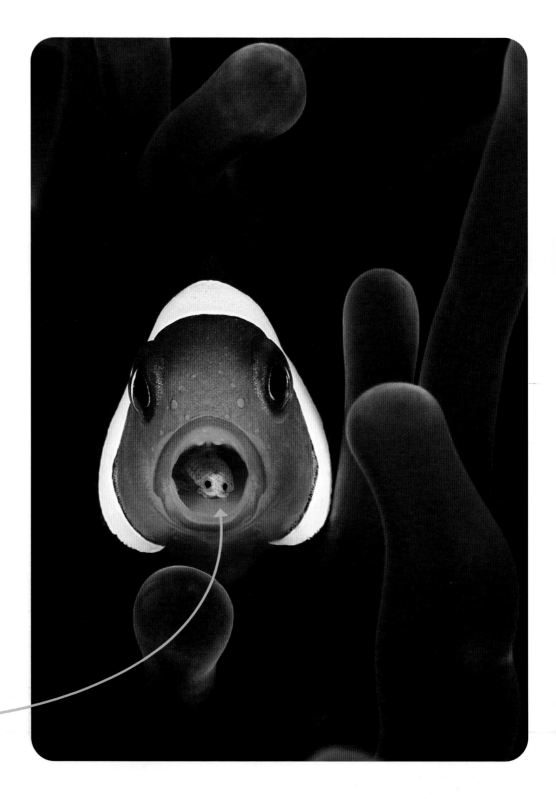

Tongue-eating louse

Berry Nice!

In the tropical forests of Central America, there's a parasitic roundworm that lives in an ant and travels in a bird. Roundworm eggs are sometimes found in the bird droppings that tree-dwelling gliding ants (*Cephalotes atratus*) collect to feed their young. (Keep reading and you'll see how they got there.) Once the ant larvae eat the egg-laden poop, the eggs hatch into worms that mate and lay hundreds of more tiny roundworm eggs, all while still inside the young ants. The newly laid eggs somehow cause the ends of the ants' abdomens to turn bright red, like berries. When the young ants leave the nest, they look enough like ripe berries to attract fruit-eating forest birds. The birds eat the infected ants, along with the roundworm eggs, and fly away. Later, they poop out the eggs in a new location. There, with luck, another gliding ant will collect the poop (with eggs) to feed to its young — and the cycle begins again.

Gliding ant (inset) infected with roundworm eggs

Zombie Nanny

The *Glyptapanteles* wasp injects its eggs into the caterpillar commonly known as an inchworm. The eggs hatch and the larvae feed on their host's body fluids while the caterpillar continues to crawl, feed and grow. Once the wasp larvae are fully developed, they eat through the inchworm's skin, attach themselves to a nearby branch or leaf and wrap themselves up in cocoons. The somewhat alive inchworm stands arched over the cocoons and behaves as though it's still under the larvae's control. If a threat approaches, the inchworm will even thrash around to drive it away. The inchworm stands guard — in zombie mode — until adult wasps crawl out of the cocoons. Only then does it die.

A Glyptapanteles wasp's eggs on a caterpillar (top) and a Glyptapanteles wasp (inset)

Grossology

So, are you grossed out yet? Some of the animals you read about *are* pretty disgusting. But they're also very successful. They have found ways to survive, reproduce and thrive that might not appeal to humans but work well for them. Once you get past the ick response — that moment when you screw up your face and turn away in disgust — you'll realize that these gross behaviors are also pretty interesting.

That's the thing about information. The more you have, the more you want. So once that ick moment and automatic disgust responses are forgotten, you'll probably find yourself wanting to know more about the fascinating creatures that share the world with us.
And *that's* thinking like a scientist!

Doing Gross Science

A lot of the science of biology is about spotting animal behavior, observing it and figuring out why it's happening. The scientists who discovered that roundworm eggs turn the abdomens of gliding ants red were studying the ants for entirely different reasons. They were curious about the red abdomens that looked like berries, dissected a few and discovered hundreds of roundworm eggs. Then they watched infected ants to see what happened to them next. What they saw were fruit-eating birds, which would never ordinarily eat an ant, flocking to the trees with the berry-like ants. From that, they figured out the rest of the process.

The trick to understanding what you observe is to ignore the grossness, whether it's an insect teeming with parasite eggs, or a stinky pile of cow poo, or an animal covered in slime. Or even a giraffe with its tongue up its nose. Instead, ask questions. You'll probably find that the more you learn, the more fascinating — and less gross — these animals will seem. And you might even make a discovery of your own.

Some Gross Extras

A **sea star** can regrow an arm (or even several arms) that's been bitten off by a predator. And bonus — some sea stars produce a protective coating of slime almost as well as hagfish do!

Rabbit regular poop

Rabbits produce two kinds of poop. During the day, they drop hard brown pellets of regular poop. At night, they produce soft, dark stuff called night feces or cecotropes (SEE-koh-trohps), which are really partly digested food. The rabbits gobble up the cecotropes to finish digesting the food they contain.

Rabbit night feces

Burrowing owls pave the tunnel to their underground nest with other animals' dung. The dung attracts beetles and small rodents that make tasty snacks for the owls. The smell of the dung might also help fool predators by disguising the scent of the nest and any baby owls.

When the dry season begins, the **West African lungfish** burrows into the soft mud left at the bottom of its swamp or stream. Then it produces a thick mucus that hardens over it to form a cozy cocoon that protects it until the rains come again.

Glossary

abdomen: the hindmost of the three segments that make up an insect's body

antenna (plural *antennae*): a sense organ located near the front of an insect's head. Also called a feeler.

artery: a blood vessel that delivers blood from the heart to the body tissues

body cavity: any space within an animal's body

colony: an organized group of insects that live together and cooperate with one another

feces: the solid bodily waste discharged from the digestive system. Also called poop.

gland: a body organ that produces chemicals

larva (plural *larvae*): the early, wingless stage of an insect's life cycle

microbe: a microscopic organism, often made of just one cell

mucus: a slimy substance produced by bodies, usually for protection and lubrication

nutrients: the substances in food that animals use to make energy and grow

organism: a life form, such as a plant, an animal or a single-celled creature

papilla (plural *papillae*): small, fleshy bumps or projections on the body of an animal or plant. For example, the bumps on your tongue are papillae.

parasite: an organism that lives on or inside a host organism and gets its food from the host

predator: an animal that eats other animals

prey: an animal that is eaten by another animal

protein: one of a group of very large molecules that are present in all living things and play a role in many different life processes

Selected Sources

Allen, Joan. "Spittlebug: A Unique Little Insect." UConn Extension, University of Connecticut, 24 July 2017, https://bugs.uconn.edu/2017/07/24/spittlebug-a-unique-little-insect/#. Accessed 28 April 2019.

"Bird-dropping spider." Australian Museum, updated 29 November 2018, https://australianmuseum.net.au/learn/animals/spiders/bird-dropping-spider/. Accessed 25 April 2019.

Blaxter, Mark, and Paul Sunnucks. "Velvet Worms." *Current Biology*, Vol. 21 Issue 7 (12 April 2011), R238-240.

Caruso, Nick, and Dani Rabaiotti. *True or Poo? The Definitive Guide to Filthy Animal Facts and Falsehoods*. New York, Boston: Hachette Books, 2018.

Chandler, David L. "How Some Beetles Produce a Scalding Defensive Spray." *MIT News*, 30 April 2015, http://news.mit.edu/2015/how-bombardier-beetles-produce-defensive-spray-0430. Accessed 18 March 2019.

Gould, Francesca, and David Haviland. *Why Dogs Eat Poop: Gross But True Things You Never Knew About Animals*. New York: G. P. Putnam's Sons, 2010.

Hewitt, Sarah. "If It Has to, a Horned Lizard Can Shoot Blood from Its Eyes." BBC Earth, 5 November 2015, http://www.bbc.com/earth/story/20151105-if-it-has-to-a-horned-lizard-can-shoot-blood-from-its-eyes. Accessed 3 April 2019.

Johnson, Nathanael. *Unseen City: The Majesty of Pigeons, the Discreet Charm of Snails & Other Wonders of the Urban Wilderness*. New York: Rodale, 2016.

Jones, Richard. *Call of Nature: The Secret Life of Dung*. Exeter, UK: Pelagic Publishing, 2017.

Palumbi, Stephen R., and Anthony R. Palumbi. *The Extreme Life of the Sea*. Princeton and Oxford: Princeton University Press, 2014.

Riley, Kathy. *Attack and Defense*. New York: Kingfisher, 2011.

Sample, Ian. "Scientists Capture Exploding Beetles' Amazing Escapes from Toads' Stomachs." *The Guardian*, 7 February 2018. https://www.theguardian.com/science/2018/feb/07/scientists-capture-exploding-beetles-amazing-escapes-from-toads-stomachs. Accessed 6 February 2018.

Senson, Pat. *Nasty, Brutish and Short: The Quirks and Quarks Guide to Animal Sex and Other Weird Behaviour*. Toronto: McClelland & Stewart, 2010.

Soares, Daphne; Adams, Rachel; Hammond, Shea; Slay, Michael E.; Fenolio, Danté B.; and Niemiller, Matthew L. "Evolution of Coprophagy and Nutrient Absorption in a Cave Salamander." *Subterranean Biology* 24: 1–9 (2017). https://doi.org/10.3897/subtbiol.24.15013. Accessed 10 April 2019.

University of California – Berkeley. "Ant Parasite Turns Host into Ripe Red Berry, Biologists Discover." *ScienceDaily*, 21 January 2008. https://www.sciencedaily.com/releases/2008/01/080116142805.htm. Accessed 12 March 2019.

University of Melbourne. "When I Grow Up, I Want to Be a Tongue." *Scientific Scribbles*, 23 August 2014. https://blogs.unimelb.edu.au/sciencecommunication/2014/08/23/when-i-grow-up-i-want-to-be-a-tongue/. Accessed 15 April 2018.

Viney, Michael. "The Snail and the Jellyfish Went to Sea." *The Irish Times*, 25 February 2017, https://www.irishtimes.com/news/environment/michael-viney-the-snail-and-the-jellyfish-went-to-sea-1.2974084. Accessed 25 March 2019.

Yong, Ed. "No One Is Prepared for Hagfish Slime." *The Atlantic*, 23 January 2019. https://amp.theatlantic.com/amp/article/581002/. Accessed 23 January 2019.

Yong, Ed. "Parrotfish Sleep in a Mosquito Net Made of Mucus." *Discover Magazine*, 17 November 2010. http://blogs.discovermagazine.com/notrocketscience/2010/11/17/parrotfish-sleep-in-a-mosquito-net-made-of-mucus/#.XS-tsvJKjIU. Accessed 12 December 2017.

Index

Ick!